WORKBOOK

THE RUTHLESS ELIMINATION OF HURRY

How to Stay Emotionally Healthy and Spiritually Alive in the Chaos of the Modern World

JOHN MARK COMER

FoxiBooks

Acknowledgement: Cover pictures designed by Freepik.com and Vecteezy.com

Note: This is an unofficial companion book to The Ruthless Elimination of Hurry written by John Mark Comer

Presented to:

Peggy Hansen

760-419-0155

From:

Mary

Sept 22, 2022

Guide to Use This Book

This book has been designed as a brainstorming tool to help bring about a positive transformation in your life as you apply the lessons from the main book into your daily life.

Each chapter has been tailored to be used alongside the corresponding chapter from the main book.

Inside this book, you would find chapter highlights and custom designed sections for self-reflection, goals, study notes and lots more...

One important aspect of this book is the section containing thought-provoking exercises/questions geared towards self-development and personal transformation.

However, in order for you to reap 100% benefits from this workbook, you need to answer each question sincerely and to the best of your ability.

For some people, they may need to purchase two copies of this book and attempt the same exercises and questions again a few weeks or months later to see if their answers would be different and what areas they have successfully improved on since the last time they worked through the book.

Take your time and work through this book and make that change you truly desire.

PROLOGUE: AUTOBIOGRAPHY OF AN EPIDEMIC

HIGHLIGHTS & KEY TAKEAWAYS

- Sometimes, you can get so busy with life that you miss out on those series of moments that make life worth living.
- You can be "successful" and still emotionally unhealthy and spiritually shallow.
- When you feel it's time, take that bold step to slow down, simplify your life and set new metrics for success.
- Value the person you are becoming over where you end up.
- Slowing down gives an opportunity for the merry-go-round blur of life to become clearer as it comes into focus.
- Look to Jesus for advice on being happy because He remains the most brilliant, insightful and thought-provoking of all the teachers throughout history.
- Life is extraordinarily complex and there's no life hack for the soul.

Answer the following questions (and remember to be sincere)

How does anxiety affect you emotionally?

paralizes me! can't think panic mode - worse as I have grown older

How does your work affect your experiences with the moments of life?

My inactively cause more anxiety.

Who are you becoming?

An old lady who sees people more than things

_____

_____

_____

_____

What would the plot of the character arc of your life look like in a few decades down the road?

less work for my girls - and hopefully will be residing in my manner with my kids in 10 years.

_____

_____

_____

_____

What are the standards you use to measure success for yourself?

Waking up in the morning acomplishing at least one task for the day

_____

_____

_____

How has these metrics changed over the years as you got older?

gone from ultra busy to slow as a snail

S.S teacher
Ministry leader
Awana Commander
Missionary —
wife - mother grandmother
friend

What steps are you willing to take to become a successful apprentice of Jesus?

Read, Study, Mediate
PRAY

Talk to my Lord
Talk to others about
my Lord

Personal Objectives and Goals After Reading This Section

_____

_____

_____

_____

_____

_____

_____

_____

_____

Outline Steps to Take to Apply the Lessons into Your Personal Life

_____

_____

_____

_____

_____

_____

_____

_____

_____

_____

Personal Insights/Reflection, Study Notes and more...

Part one

The problem

HURRY: THE GREAT ENEMY OF SPIRITUAL LIFE

HIGHLIGHTS & KEY TAKEAWAYS

- Hurry is a major enemy of the spiritual life of Christians today.
- In our world today, at the root of so many symptoms of toxicity are the problem of hurry.
- The devil is far more intelligent than we tend to give him credit for.
- Having too much to do is the problem and not having a lot to do. Hurry tends to come in when you have too much to do.
- Jesus said love is the greatest command, however, love is not compatible with hurry.
- Love, joy and peace are the overall conditions of the heart and not mere emotions or pleasant feelings.
- Hurry steals your attention and keeps you away from God.

Answer the following questions (and remember to be sincere)

Before reading John Comer's book, what would you say is the greatest enemy of your spiritual life?

_____

_____

_____

_____

_____

_____

_____

_____

_____

_____

What is the relationship between sin and busyness?

_____

_____

_____

_____

_____

_____

_____

_____

_____

When can busyness be classified as healthy?

_____

_____

_____

_____

_____

_____

_____

Why is busyness a major distraction from spiritual life?

_____

_____

_____

_____

_____

_____

_____

What are those traits you exhibit when you are in a hurry?

_____

_____

_____

_____

_____

_____

_____

What is that activity you often engage in that forces you to slow down? (For pastor John, it was reading poetry)

_____

_____

_____

_____

_____

Personal Objectives and Goals After Reading This Section

_____

_____

_____

_____

_____

_____

_____

_____

Outline Steps to Take to Apply the Lessons into Your Personal Life

_____

_____

_____

_____

_____

_____

_____

_____

_____

Personal Insights/Reflection, Study Notes and more...

A BRIEF HISTORY OF SPEED

HIGHLIGHTS & KEY TAKEAWAYS

- The arrival of the clock created artificial time, made us more efficient, but more machine and less human.
- In America, sleep time has reduced by around two and a half hours from a century ago, and this could be the reason for constant exhaustion.
- Technological advances have changed the way we relate with time, yet, some of us still feel we have less time even with all the quicker ways of doing things that technology has afforded us.
- Whether they are turned on or off, our smartphones have an impact on our working memory, concentration, problem solving skills, etc.
- When companies get your attention, they get your money.

Answer the following questions (and remember to be sincere)

Why is the clock a far more demanding master than the sun?

_____

_____

_____

_____

_____

_____

_____

_____

_____

_____

How does busyness relate to wealth in our world today?

_____

_____

_____

_____

_____

_____

_____

_____

How can we, as a society, reduce the negative effects of the internet?

_____

_____

_____

_____

_____

_____

_____

_____
_____
_____
_____

How much time do you lose to your smart phone every day?
Give a rough estimate?

_____
_____
_____
_____
_____
_____
_____

Are there any steps you can take to reduce the average
time you spend on your smartphone every day?

_____
_____
_____
_____
_____
_____
_____

_____
_____

Would you consider yourself to be addicted to your phone?

_____
_____
_____
_____
_____
_____
_____
_____
_____
_____

How much value do you place on your attention?

_____
_____
_____
_____
_____
_____
_____
_____
_____
_____
_____

Personal Objectives and Goals After Reading This Section

_____
_____
_____
_____
_____
_____
_____
_____

Outline Steps to Take to Apply the Lessons into Your Personal Life

_____
_____
_____
_____
_____
_____
_____
_____
_____

Personal Insights/Reflection, Study Notes and more...

_____

_____

_____

_____

_____

_____

_____

_____

_____

_____

_____

_____

_____

_____

_____

_____

_____

_____

_____

_____

_____

_____

_____

_____

_____

_____

_____

SOMETHING IS DEEPLY WRONG

HIGHLIGHTS & KEY TAKEAWAYS

- Our life speed has been labeled a disease and is becoming out of control and dangerous.
- Pastor John outlined ten symptoms of hurry sickness to include; irritability, hypersensitivity, restlessness, workaholism, emotional numbness, out-of-order priorities, lack of care for your body, escapist behavior, slippage of spiritual disciplines and isolation.
- Even though it's the new normal in the Western world, a hurried life is toxic.
- Hurry threatens your emotional and spiritual life.

Answer the following questions (and remember to be sincere)

According to the context of this section of the main book, how do you recognize when you need to restore life?

_____

_____

_____

_____

_____

_____

_____

_____

How would you know if you or someone else has hurry sickness?

_____

_____

_____

_____

_____

_____

What are the symptoms of hurry sickness you can identify in your own life? Use the ten symptoms from the main text as a guide.

_____

_____

_____

_____

_____

_____

How do you handle those moments when you feel so stressed and distracted?

_____

_____

_____

_____

_____

_____

_____

_____

_____

_____

What are those things you hold dear that you feel you
have lost as a result of hurry?

_____

_____

_____

_____

_____

_____

What are you giving your attention to and how is this
affecting the person you are becoming?

_____

_____

_____

_____

_____

_____

_____

_____

Personal Objectives and Goals After Reading This Section

_____

_____

_____

_____

_____

_____

_____

_____

_____

Outline Steps to Take to Apply the Lessons into Your Personal Life

_____

_____

_____

_____

_____

_____

_____

_____

_____

_____

Part Two

The Solution

HINT: THE SOLUTION ISN'T MORE TIME

HIGHLIGHTS & KEY TAKEAWAYS

- Slow down and simplify your life. Focus on those things that really matter because that's the solution to an overbusy life.
- You need to live into both your potential, and your limitation.
- In our world today, people find it difficult accepting their limitations.
- When you live a life of comparison, it eats your joy.
- Your limitation can be a pathway to finding God's will for your life.
- Sometimes, you're just too distracted to do what you know is important.

Answer the following questions (and remember to be sincere)

What do you think would be the outcome if you were given more time in the day?

_____

_____

_____

_____

_____

_____

_____

_____

_____

_____

_____

Use the space below to list out those things that really matter in your life

_____

_____

_____

_____

_____

_____

How willing are you to accept your limitations?

_____

_____

_____

_____

_____

_____

_____

_____

_____

_____

What are those limitations that you find hard to accept?

_____

_____

_____

_____

_____

_____

_____

_____

Discuss or outline your personal strategy to live
deliberately

_____

_____

_____

_____

_____

_____

_____

_____

_____

_____

_____

_____

Personal Objectives and Goals After Reading This Section

_____
_____
_____
_____
_____
_____
_____
_____
_____

Outline Steps to Take to Apply the Lessons into Your Personal Life

_____
_____
_____
_____
_____
_____
_____
_____
_____

THE SECRET OF THE EASY YOKE

HIGHLIGHTS & KEY TAKEAWAYS

- To be one of Jesus' apprentices, you need to be with Jesus, become like Him and do what He would do if He were you.
- Salvation is healing to your soul
- Through apprenticeship, we can find healing in Jesus.
- Adopt the lifestyle of Jesus so that you can experience His life.

Answer the following questions (and remember to be sincere)

For you, what's the correlation between hurry and spirituality?

_____

_____

_____

_____

_____

_____

_____

_____

_____

_____

_____

_____

_____

_____

_____

How much effort have you put into trying to model your life
after Jesus?

_____

_____

_____

_____

_____

_____

_____

_____

_____

How would you train/teach your children (or younger family
member or friend) to model their lives after Jesus?

_____

_____

_____

_____

_____

_____

_____

_____

_____

_____

_____

Do you feel a little burned out on religion?

_____

_____

_____

_____

_____

_____

Why do you think Jesus as the truth is more popular and gets more attention than Jesus as the way?

_____

_____

_____

_____

_____

_____

_____

_____

_____

Personal Objectives and Goals After Reading This Section

_____

_____

_____

_____

_____

_____

_____

_____

_____

Outline Steps to Take to Apply the Lessons into Your Personal Life

_____

_____

_____

_____

_____

_____

_____

_____

_____

WHAT WE'RE REALLY TALKING ABOUT IS A RULE OF LIFE

HIGHLIGHTS & KEY TAKEAWAYS

- Jesus was fiercely present and not in a hurry with life.
- Like Jesus, you need to be firmly rooted in the moment and connected to God, other people and yourself.
- Aligning your schedule to your values is a pathway for inner peace.
- Most times, the problem is not the lack of time but simply the allocation of it. We need to reallocate our time to seek God's kingdom and not the social media or TV entertainments.

Answer the following questions (and remember to be sincere)

How would you handle your "full schedule" and at the same time, not come off as hurried?

_____
_____
_____
_____
_____
_____
_____
_____

_____

_____

_____

_____

How would you describe your connection to God and people around you?

_____

_____

_____

_____

_____

_____

_____

_____

_____

What does living "freely and lightly" mean to you?

_____

_____

_____

_____

_____

_____

_____

_____

_____
_____
_____
_____

What should be your top priorities in order to live an
unhurried life?

_____
_____
_____
_____
_____
_____
_____
_____
_____

How do you think Jesus would live if He were you?

_____
_____
_____
_____
_____
_____
_____
_____

_____

_____

_____

_____

_____

What are the necessary structures you need to put in place
to facilitate the health and growth of your life with Jesus?

_____

_____

_____

_____

_____

_____

_____

_____

_____

Are you ready to radically rethink your schedule in order
to make Jesus' life become your new normal?

_____

_____

_____

_____

_____

_____

_____

Personal Objectives and Goals After Reading This Section

_____

_____

_____

_____

_____

_____

_____

_____

Outline Steps to Take to Apply the Lessons into Your Personal Life

_____

_____

_____

_____

_____

_____

_____

_____

_____

PART THREE

Four Practices for
Unhurrying Your Life

SILENCE AND SOLITUDE

HIGHLIGHTS & KEY TAKEAWAYS

- The arrival of the digital age made us more efficient than ever, with more things being done in much lesser time.
- You are being robbed of the ability to be present by the hurried digital distraction which now seems to be the new normal in our society today.
- The noise from the world we live in today drowns out God's voice and input from our lives.
- Your ability to pay attention is crucial for your spiritual growth.
- When life becomes hectic, make your quiet place your first go to.
- Quiet is important for emotional healing.
- Andrew Sullivan opines that the greatest threat to faith today is distraction.

Answer the following questions (and remember to be sincere)

How much effect has the digital age had on your relationship with God and your apprenticeship with Jesus?

_____
_____
_____
_____

_____
_____
_____
_____
_____
_____
_____
_____
_____

How often do you wake up to the reality of God in your daily life?

_____
_____
_____
_____
_____
_____
_____
_____

When nothing is taking your attention, what is the first thing you do?

_____
_____
_____

_____

_____

_____

_____

_____

_____

_____

_____

_____

_____

Outline some of your excuses why you can't have your quiet place in those overbusy and hectic seasons?

_____

_____

_____

_____

_____

_____

_____

_____

_____

_____

_____

_____

_____

_____

_____

_____

_____

_____

_____

_____

What steps would you take to have frequent quiet times
with God?

_____

_____

_____

_____

_____

_____

_____

_____

How do you open yourself up to God and enjoy Him?

_____

_____

_____

_____

_____

_____

_____

_____

_____

Personal Objectives and Goals After Reading This Section

_____

_____

_____

_____

_____

_____

_____

_____

_____

Outline Steps to Take to Apply the Lessons into Your Personal Life

_____

_____

_____

_____

_____

_____

_____

_____

_____

Personal Insights/Reflection, Study Notes and more...

_____
_____
_____
_____
_____
_____
_____
_____
_____
_____
_____
_____
_____
_____
_____
_____
_____
_____
_____
_____
_____
_____
_____
_____

SABBATH

HIGHLIGHTS & KEY TAKEAWAYS

- Do not allow desire drive your life beyond your control.
- As humans, we are finite while our desires are infinite, and this leads to restlessness.
- As apprentices of Jesus, we need to put our desire back on God.
- Only God can satisfy our desires.
- Advertisers seek to monetize your restlessness
- Sabbath is a spirit of restfulness and a state of being.
- The Sabbath is blessed by God and has life-giving capacity.

Answer the following questions (and remember to be sincere)

Do you believe your desire can ever be satisfied? Give reasons for your answer?

_____

_____

_____

_____

_____

_____

_____

_____

Presently, what do you think you need in order to live a happy, restful life?

_____
_____
_____
_____
_____
_____
_____
_____

What are the consequences of an unending pursuit of your desires?

_____
_____
_____
_____
_____
_____
_____
_____
_____
_____
_____
_____

How much gratitude and contentment do you have for your life?

_____
_____
_____
_____
_____
_____
_____
_____
_____
_____
_____

Reflect on your life and decide whether you belong to the restfulness category, or the relentlessness category.

_____
_____
_____
_____
_____
_____
_____
_____
_____
_____

After going through this section, what does the Sabbath mean to you?

_____

_____

_____

_____

_____

_____

_____

_____

_____

_____

_____

Why is the Sabbath necessary for you as an apprentice of Jesus?

_____

_____

_____

_____

_____

_____

_____

_____

_____

Personal Objectives and Goals After Reading This Section

_____

_____

_____

_____

_____

_____

_____

_____

_____

_____

Outline Steps to Take to Apply the Lessons into Your Personal Life

_____

_____

_____

_____

_____

_____

_____

_____

_____

_____

SIMPLICITY

HIGHLIGHTS & KEY TAKEAWAYS

- Shopping has usurped the place of religion in America
- Humans are desire-driven, making them easily emotionally tricked.
- Your wants are not actually needs.
- Adverts are designed to fuel the fire of desires in our bellies
- We have an insatiable desire for more and believe our happiness lies in having more things, when in fact, we need very few.
- The most important things in life are not material things, rather, they are the relationships you build with God, your family and friends.
- Simplicity is highly focused on only those things that matter most and add value to your life

Answer the following questions (and remember to be sincere)

How does money affect your relationship and fellowship with God?

_____

_____

_____

_____

_____

_____

_____

_____

_____

_____

_____

_____

_____

What are your thoughts on materialism in the Western world?

_____

_____

_____

_____

_____

_____

_____

_____

What gives meaning to your life?

_____

_____

_____

_____

_____

_____

_____

_____

_____

_____

_____

_____

_____

What is that lie you have believed about the relationship between money and happiness?

_____

_____

_____

_____

_____

_____

_____

_____

_____

Do you believe you can adjust your life towards simplicity?

_____

_____

_____

_____

_____

_____

_____

_____

_____

_____

Make a list of your five most recent significant purchases, and next to each, write the true cost (both in cash and time) and if it sped up or slowed down your life.

_____

_____

_____

_____

_____

_____

_____

_____

_____

_____

_____

_____

_____

_____

_____

_____

_____

How do you intend to implement the 12 principles from this section of the main book?

_____

_____

_____

_____

_____

_____

_____

_____

_____

_____

_____

_____

_____

_____

_____

_____

_____

_____

_____

_____

_____

_____

_____

_____

_____

_____

_____

_____

Personal Objectives and Goals After Reading This Section

_____

_____

_____

_____

_____

_____

_____

_____

Outline Steps to Take to Apply the Lessons into Your Personal Life

_____

_____

_____

_____

_____

_____

_____

_____

_____

SLOWING

HIGHLIGHTS & KEY TAKEAWAYS

- You would achieve inner peace when your schedules and values are aligned.
- Your thinking influences how your experience with God would be.
- Enjoy life without feeling the need to increase in speed.

Answer the following questions (and remember to be sincere)

Which of the 20 rules, from the main book, would you begin to implement?

_____

_____

_____

_____

_____

_____

_____

_____

_____

_____

_____

_____

_____

_____

_____

_____

_____

_____

_____

_____

_____

Which of the 20 rules do you see yourself never implementing? Why?

_____

_____

_____

_____

_____

_____

_____

_____

_____

_____

_____

_____

_____

_____

_____

_____

_____

_____

_____

_____

What do you thinking would be your limitation in implementing these rules?

_____

_____

_____

_____

_____

_____

_____

_____

_____

_____

_____

_____

_____

_____

_____

_____

_____

In the space below, come up with your own list of things to do or rules to follow in order to help you slow down your speed in life.

_____

_____

_____

_____

_____

_____

_____

_____

_____

_____

_____

_____

_____

_____

_____

_____

_____

_____

_____

_____

_____

_____

_____

_____

_____

_____

_____

_____

_____

_____

_____

What other ways have you tried to identify and deal with
the hurry in your soul?

_____

_____

_____

_____

_____

_____

_____

_____

_____

_____

_____

_____

_____

_____

_____

_____

Personal Objectives and Goals After Reading This Section

_____
_____
_____
_____
_____
_____
_____
_____
_____

Outline Steps to Take to Apply the Lessons into Your Personal Life

_____
_____
_____
_____
_____
_____
_____
_____
_____

Personal Insights/Reflection, Study Notes and more...

_____
_____
_____
_____
_____
_____
_____
_____
_____
_____
_____
_____
_____
_____
_____
_____
_____
_____
_____
_____
_____
_____
_____
_____
_____
_____
_____
_____
_____
_____
_____

Made in the USA
Las Vegas, NV
17 September 2022

55475727R00044